# Duncan Hines®

# CLASSIC RECIPES™

Publications International, Ltd.

Favorite Brand Name Recipes at www.fbnr.com

**Microwave Cooking:** Microwave ovens vary in wattage. Use the cooking times as
guidelines and check for doneness before adding more time.

# Table of Contents

Chocolate Obsession     6

Collectible Cookies     30

Cakes, Breads & More     52

Index     76

# Chocolate Obsession

Nothing is more sensuous or satisfying than chocolate. Go ahead and indulge your cravings with this incredible assortment of treats from tortes to truffles. Duncan Hines® makes luscious chocolate desserts a piece of cake.

# Chocolate Peanut Butter Cups

1 package DUNCAN HINES® Moist Deluxe® Swiss Chocolate
 Cake Mix
1 container DUNCAN HINES® Creamy Home-Style Classic
 Vanilla Frosting
$^1/_2$ cup creamy peanut butter
15 miniature peanut butter cup candies, wrappers removed, cut in
 half vertically

1. Preheat oven to 350°F. Place 30 ($2^1/_2$-inch) paper liners in muffin cups.

2. Prepare, bake and cool cupcakes following package directions for basic recipe.

3. Combine vanilla frosting and peanut butter in medium bowl. Stir until smooth. Frost one cupcake. Decorate with peanut butter cup candy, cut side down. Repeat with remaining cupcakes, frosting and candies.

*Makes 30 servings*

**Tip:** You may substitute Duncan Hines® Moist Deluxe® Devil's Food, Dark Chocolate Fudge or Butter Recipe Fudge Cake Mix flavors for Swiss Chocolate Cake Mix.

# Upside-Down German Chocolate Cake

1¹/₂ cups flaked coconut

1¹/₂ cups chopped pecans

1 package DUNCAN HINES® Moist Deluxe® German Chocolate or Classic Chocolate Cake Mix

1 package (8 ounces) cream cheese, softened

¹/₂ cup butter or margarine, melted

1 pound (3¹/₂ to 4 cups) confectioners' sugar

1. Preheat oven to 350°F. Grease and flour 13×9-inch pan.

2. Spread coconut evenly on bottom of prepared pan. Sprinkle with pecans. Prepare cake mix as directed on package. Pour over coconut and pecans. Combine cream cheese and melted butter in medium mixing bowl. Beat at low speed with electric mixer until creamy. Add sugar; beat until blended and smooth. Drop by spoonfuls evenly over cake batter. Bake at 350°F for 45 to 50 minutes or until toothpick inserted halfway to bottom of cake comes out clean. Cool completely in pan. To serve, cut into individual pieces; turn upside down onto plate.

*Makes 12 to 16 servings*

**Tip:** This cake can be served warm, if desired. Also, store leftover coconut in the refrigerator and use within four weeks.

*Upside-Down German Chocolate Cake*

# Chocolate Cherry Torte

1 package DUNCAN HINES® Moist Deluxe® Devil's Food
    Cake Mix
1 can (21 ounces) cherry pie filling
$1/4$ teaspoon almond extract
1 container (8 ounces) frozen whipped topping, thawed and
    divided
$1/4$ cup toasted sliced almonds, for garnish (see Tip)

1. Preheat oven to 350°F. Grease and flour two 9-inch round cake pans.

2. Prepare, bake and cool cake following package directions for basic recipe. Combine cherry pie filling and almond extract in small bowl. Stir until blended.

3. To assemble, place one cake layer on serving plate. Spread with 1 cup whipped topping, then half the cherry pie filling mixture. Top with second cake layer. Spread remaining pie filling to within $1^1/2$ inches of cake edge. Decorate cake edge with remaining whipped topping. Garnish with sliced almonds.                     *Makes 12 to 16 servings*

**Tip:** To toast almonds, spread in a single layer on baking sheet. Bake at 325°F 4 to 6 minutes or until fragrant and golden.

*Chocolate Cherry Torte*

# Chocolate Streusel Cake

STREUSEL

    1 package DUNCAN HINES® Moist Deluxe® Devil's Food
        Cake Mix, divided

    1 cup finely chopped pecans

    2 tablespoons brown sugar

    2 teaspoons ground cinnamon

CAKE

    3 eggs

  1$^1/_3$ cups water

    $^1/_2$ cup vegetable oil

TOPPING

    1 container (8 ounces) frozen whipped topping, thawed

    3 tablespoons sifted unsweetened cocoa powder

    Chopped pecans for garnish (optional)

    Chocolate curls for garnish (optional)

1. Preheat oven to 350°F. Grease and flour 10-inch Bundt pan.

2. For streusel, combine 2 tablespoons cake mix, 1 cup pecans, brown sugar and cinnamon. Set aside.

3. For cake, combine remaining cake mix, eggs, water and oil in large bowl. Beat at medium speed with electric mixer for 2 minutes. Pour two-thirds of batter into prepared pan. Sprinkle with reserved streusel. Pour remaining batter evenly over streusel. Bake at 350°F for 55 to 60 minutes or until toothpick inserted in center comes out clean. Cool in pan 25 minutes. Invert onto serving plate. Cool completely.

**4.** For topping, place whipped topping in medium bowl. Fold in cocoa until blended. Spread on cooled cake. Garnish with chopped pecans and chocolate curls, if desired. Refrigerate until ready to serve.

*Makes 12 to 16 servings*

**Tip:** For chocolate curls, warm chocolate in microwave oven at HIGH (100% power) for 5 to 10 seconds. Make chocolate curls by holding a sharp vegetable peeler against the flat side of a chocolate block and bringing the blade toward you. Apply firm pressure for thicker, more open curls or light pressure for tighter curls.

*Chocolate Streusel Cake*

# Banana Fudge Layer Cake

1 package DUNCAN HINES® Moist Deluxe® Yellow Cake Mix
1 1/3 cups water
3 eggs
1/3 cup vegetable oil
1 cup mashed ripe bananas (about 3 medium)
1 container DUNCAN HINES® Chocolate Frosting

1. Preheat oven to 350°F. Grease and flour two 9-inch round cake pans.

2. Combine cake mix, water, eggs and oil in large bowl. Beat at low speed with electric mixer until moistened. Beat at medium speed 2 minutes. Stir in bananas.

3. Pour into prepared pans. Bake at 350°F for 28 to 31 minutes or until toothpick inserted in center comes out clean. Cool in pans 15 minutes. Remove from pans; cool completely.

4. Fill and frost cake with frosting. Garnish as desired.

*Makes 12 to 16 servings*

*Banana Fudge Layer Cake*

# Chocolate Almond Confection Cake

CAKE

    1 package (7 ounces) pure almond paste
    1/2 cup vegetable oil, divided plus additional for greasing
    3 eggs
    1 package DUNCAN HINES® Moist Deluxe® Devil's Food
        Cake Mix
  1 1/3 cups water

GLAZE

    1 package (6 ounces) semisweet chocolate chips
    3 tablespoons cherry jelly or seedless red raspberry jam
    2 tablespoons butter or margarine
    1 tablespoon light corn syrup
      Natural sliced almonds, for garnish
      Candied whole maraschino cherries or fresh raspberries,
        for garnish

1. Preheat oven to 350°F. Grease and flour 10-inch Bundt or tube pan.

2. For cake, combine almond paste and 2 tablespoons oil in large bowl. Beat at medium speed with electric mixer until blended. Add remaining oil, 2 tablespoons at a time, until blended. Add 1 egg; beat at medium speed until blended. Add remaining 2 eggs; beat until smooth. Add cake mix and water; beat at medium speed for 2 minutes. Pour into pan. Bake at 350°F for 50 to 55 minutes or until toothpick inserted in center comes out clean. Cool in pan 25 minutes. Invert onto cooling rack. Cool completely.

3. For glaze, place chocolate chips, cherry jelly, butter and corn syrup in microwave-safe medium bowl. Microwave at HIGH (100% power) for 1 to $1^1/2$ minutes. Stir until melted and smooth. Glaze top of cake. Garnish with sliced almonds and maraschino cherries.

*Makes 12 to 16 servings*

**Tip:** This recipe may also be prepared in the food processor. Place almond paste in work bowl with knife blade. Process until finely chopped. Add cake mix, eggs, water and oil. Process for 1 minute or until smooth. Bake and cool as directed above.

# Truffles

1 container DUNCAN HINES® Creamy Home-Style
   Milk Chocolate Frosting
$2^1/2$ cups confectioners' sugar
1 cup pecan halves, divided
1 cup semisweet chocolate chips
3 tablespoons shortening

1. Combine frosting and sugar in large mixing bowl. Stir with wooden spoon until thoroughly blended. Chop $^1/3$ cup pecan halves; set aside. Cover remaining pecan halves with 1 tablespoon frosting mixture each.

2. Place chocolate chips and shortening in 2-cup glass measuring cup. Microwave at MEDIUM (50% power) for 2 minutes; stir. Microwave 1 minute at MEDIUM; stir until smooth. Dip one pecan ball into chocolate mixture until completely covered. Remove with fork to cooling rack. Sprinkle top with chopped pecans. Repeat until all candy balls are covered. Allow to stand until chocolate mixture is set.

*Makes about 3 dozen candies*

# Double Chocolate Chewies

1 package DUNCAN HINES® Moist Deluxe® Butter Recipe
   Fudge Cake Mix

2 eggs

$^1/_2$ cup butter or margarine, melted

1 package (6 ounces) semisweet chocolate chips

1 cup chopped nuts

Confectioners' sugar (optional)

1. Preheat oven to 350°F. Grease 13×9×2-inch pan.

2. Combine cake mix, eggs and melted butter in large bowl. Stir until
thoroughly blended. (Mixture will be stiff.) Stir in chocolate chips and
nuts. Press mixture evenly in prepared pan. Bake at 350°F for 25 to
30 minutes or until toothpick inserted in center comes out clean. *Do not
overbake.* Cool completely. Cut into bars. Dust with confectioners' sugar, if
desired.                                                   *Makes 36 bars*

**Tip:** For a special effect, cut a paper towel into $^1/_4$-inch-wide strips. Place
strips in diagonal pattern on top of cooled bars before cutting. Place
confectioners' sugar in tea strainer. Tap strainer lightly to dust surface
with sugar. Carefully remove strips.

*Double Chocolate Chewies*

# Chocolate Chip Cheesecake

1 package DUNCAN HINES® Moist Deluxe® Devil's Food
Cake Mix
1/2 cup vegetable oil
3 packages (8 ounces each) cream cheese, softened
1 1/2 cups granulated sugar
1 cup sour cream
1 1/2 teaspoons vanilla extract
4 eggs, lightly beaten
3/4 cup mini semisweet chocolate chips, divided
1 teaspoon all-purpose flour

1. Preheat oven to 350°F. Grease 10-inch springform pan.

2. Combine cake mix and oil in large bowl. Mix well. Press onto bottom of prepared pan. Bake at 350°F for 22 to 25 minutes or until set. Remove from oven. *Increase oven temperature to 450°F.*

3. Place cream cheese in large mixing bowl. Beat at low speed with electric mixer, adding sugar gradually. Add sour cream and vanilla extract, mixing until blended. Add eggs, mixing only until incorporated. Toss 1/2 cup chocolate chips with flour. Fold into cream cheese mixture. Pour filling onto crust. Sprinkle with remaining 1/4 cup chocolate chips. Bake at 450°F for 5 to 7 minutes. *Reduce oven temperature to 250°F.* Bake at 250°F for 60 to 65 minutes or until set. Loosen cake from side of pan with knife or spatula. Cool completely in pan on cooling rack. Refrigerate until ready to serve. Remove side of pan.          *Makes 12 to 16 servings*

**Tip:** Place pan of water on bottom shelf of oven during baking to prevent cheesecake from cracking.

*Chocolate Chip Cheesecake*

# Coconut Chocolate Chip Loaf

1 package DUNCAN HINES® Bakery-Style Chocolate Chip
    Muffin Mix

$1^{1}/_{3}$ cups toasted flaked coconut (see Tip)

$^{3}/_{4}$ cup water

1 egg

$^{1}/_{2}$ teaspoon vanilla extract

Confectioners' sugar for garnish (optional)

1. Preheat oven to 350°F. Grease and flour 9×5×3-inch loaf pan.

2. Empty muffin mix into medium bowl. Break up any lumps. Add
coconut, water, egg and vanilla extract. Stir until moistened, about
50 strokes. Pour into prepared pan. Bake at 350°F for 45 to 50 minutes
or until toothpick inserted in center comes out clean. Cool in pan
15 minutes. Invert onto cooling rack. Turn right side up. Cool completely.
Dust with confectioners' sugar, if desired.    *Makes 1 loaf (12 slices)*

**Tip:** Spread coconut evenly on baking sheet. Toast at 350°F for
5 minutes. Stir and toast 1 to 2 minutes longer or until light golden
brown.

*Coconut Chocolate Chip Loaf*

# Triple Chocolate Fantasy

CAKE

  1 package DUNCAN HINES® Moist Deluxe® Devil's Food
    Cake Mix

  3 eggs

  1 1/3 cups water

  1/2 cup vegetable oil plus additional for greasing

  1/2 cup ground walnuts

CHOCOLATE GLAZE

  1 package (12 ounces) semisweet chocolate chips

  1/4 cup plus 2 tablespoons butter or margarine

  1/4 cup coarsely chopped walnuts

WHITE CHOCOLATE GLAZE

  3 ounces white chocolate, coarsely chopped

  1 tablespoon shortening

1. Preheat oven to 350°F. Grease and flour 10-inch Bundt pan.

2. For cake, combine cake mix, eggs, water, oil and ground walnuts in large bowl. Beat at medium speed with electric mixer for 2 minutes. Pour into prepared pan. Bake at 350°F for 45 to 55 minutes or until toothpick inserted in center comes out clean. Cool in pan 25 minutes. Invert onto serving plate. Cool completely.

3. For chocolate glaze, combine chocolate chips and butter in small heavy saucepan. Heat on low heat until chips are melted. Stir constantly until shiny and smooth. (Glaze will be very thick.) Spread hot glaze over cooled cake. Sprinkle with coarsely chopped walnuts.

**4.** For white chocolate glaze, combine white chocolate and shortening in small heavy saucepan. Heat on low heat until melted, stirring constantly. Drizzle hot glaze over top and sides of cake. *Makes 12 to 16 servings*

# Cindy's Fudgy Brownies

1 (21-ounce) package DUNCAN HINES® Family-Style Chewy
    Fudge Brownie Mix

1 egg

$^1/_3$ cup water

$^1/_3$ cup vegetable oil

$^3/_4$ cup semisweet chocolate chips

$^1/_2$ cup chopped pecans

**1.** Preheat oven to 350°F. Grease bottom only of 13×9×2-inch pan.

**2.** Combine brownie mix, egg, water and oil in large bowl. Stir with spoon until well blended, about 50 strokes. Stir in chocolate chips. Spread in prepared pan. Sprinkle with pecans. Bake at 350°F for 25 to 28 minutes or until set. Cool completely. Cut into bars. *Makes 24 brownies*

**Tip:** Overbaking brownies will cause them to become dry. Follow the recommended baking times given in recipes closely.

# Chocolate Toffee Crunch Fantasy

1 package DUNCAN HINES® Moist Deluxe® Devil's Food
   Cake Mix
12 bars (1.4 ounces each) chocolate covered toffee bars, divided
3 cups whipping cream, chilled

1. Preheat oven to 350°F. Grease and flour 10-inch tube pan.

2. Prepare, bake and cool cake following package directions. Split cake horizontally into three layers; set aside. Chop 11 candy bars into pea-size pieces (see Tip). Whip cream until stiff peaks form. Fold candy pieces into whipped cream.

3. To assemble, place one split cake layer on serving plate. Spread 1½ cups whipped cream mixture on top. Repeat with remaining layers and whipped cream mixture. Frost sides and top with remaining filling. Chop remaining candy bar coarsely. Sprinkle over top. Refrigerate until ready to serve.                    *Makes 12 servings*

**Tip:** To quickly chop toffee candy bars, place a few bars in food processor fitted with steel blade. Pulse several times until pea-size pieces form. Repeat with remaining candy bars.

*Chocolate Toffee Crunch Fantasy*

# Chocolate Cream Torte

1 package DUNCAN HINES® Moist Deluxe® Devil's Food
    Cake Mix
1 package (8 ounces) cream cheese, softened
$^1/_2$ cup sugar
1 teaspoon vanilla extract
1 cup finely chopped pecans
1 cup whipping cream, chilled
    Strawberry halves for garnish
    Mint leaves for garnish

1. Preheat oven to 350°F. Grease and flour two 8- or 9-inch round cake pans.

2. Prepare, bake and cool cake following package directions for basic recipe. Chill layers for ease in splitting.

3. Place cream cheese, sugar and vanilla extract in small bowl. Beat at low speed with electric mixer until smooth. Add pecans; stir until blended. Set aside. Beat whipping cream in small bowl until stiff peaks form. Fold whipped cream into cream cheese mixture.

4. To assemble, split each cake layer in half horizontally (see Tip). Place one cake layer on serving plate. Spread top with one fourth of filling. Repeat with remaining layers and filling. Garnish with strawberry halves and mint leaves, if desired. Refrigerate until ready to serve.

*Makes 12 to 16 servings*

**Tip:** To split layers evenly, measure cake with ruler. Divide into 2 equal layers. Mark with toothpicks. Cut through layers with serrated knife, using toothpicks as guide.

*Chocolate Cream Torte*

# Collectible Cookies

Whether they're chewy or crisp, round or rectangular, cookies bring a smile to everyone's face. With Duncan Hines® mixes it's so easy to make the family's favorite treats, you may never have an empty cookie jar again.

# Chocolate Oat Chewies

1 package DUNCAN HINES® Moist Deluxe® Devil's Food
    Cake Mix
1⅓ cups old-fashioned oats, uncooked
1 cup flaked coconut, toasted and divided
¾ cup butter or margarine, melted
2 eggs, beaten
1 teaspoon vanilla extract
5 bars (1.55 ounces each) milk chocolate, cut into rectangles

1. Preheat oven to 350°F.

2. Combine cake mix, oats, ½ cup coconut, butter, eggs and vanilla extract in large bowl. Cover and chill 15 minutes.

3. Shape dough into 1-inch balls. Place balls 2 inches apart on ungreased baking sheets. Bake at 350°F for 12 minutes or until tops are slightly cracked. Remove from oven. Press one milk chocolate rectangle into center of each cookie. Sprinkle with remaining ½ cup coconut. Remove to cooling racks. *Makes about 4½ dozen cookies*

# Pinwheel Cookies

$^1/_2$ cup shortening plus additional for greasing
$^1/_3$ cup plus 1 tablespoon butter, softened and divided
  2 egg yolks
$^1/_2$ teaspoon vanilla extract
  1 package DUNCAN HINES® Moist Deluxe® Fudge Marble
     Cake Mix

1. Combine $^1/_2$ cup shortening, $^1/_3$ cup butter, egg yolks and vanilla extract in large bowl. Mix at low speed of electric mixer until blended. Set aside cocoa packet from cake mix. Gradually add cake mix. Blend well.

2. Divide dough in half. Add cocoa packet and remaining 1 tablespoon butter to one half of dough. Knead until well blended and chocolate colored.

3. Roll out yellow dough between two pieces of waxed paper into 18×12×1/8-inch rectangle. Repeat for chocolate dough. Remove top pieces of waxed paper from chocolate and yellow doughs. Place yellow dough directly on top of chocolate dough. Remove remaining layers of waxed paper. Roll up jelly-roll fashion, beginning at wide side. Refrigerate 2 hours.

4. Preheat oven to 350°F. Grease baking sheets.

5. Cut dough into $^1/_8$-inch slices. Place sliced dough 1 inch apart on prepared baking sheets. Bake at 350°F for 9 to 11 minutes or until lightly browned. Cool 5 minutes on baking sheets. Remove to cooling racks.                               *Makes about 3$^1/_2$ dozen cookies*

*Pinwheel Cookies*

# Cinnamon Stars

2 tablespoons sugar

³/₄ teaspoon ground cinnamon

³/₄ cup butter or margarine, softened

2 egg yolks

1 teaspoon vanilla extract

1 package DUNCAN HINES® Moist Deluxe® French Vanilla
Cake Mix

1. Preheat oven to 375°F. Combine sugar and cinnamon in small bowl.
Set aside.

2. Combine butter, egg yolks and vanilla extract in large bowl. Blend in
cake mix gradually. Roll dough to ¹/₈-inch thickness on lightly floured
surface. Cut with 2¹/₂-inch star cookie cutter. Place 2 inches apart on
ungreased baking sheet.

3. Sprinkle cookies with cinnamon-sugar mixture. Bake at 375°F for
6 to 8 minutes or until edges are light golden brown. Cool 1 minute on
baking sheet. Remove to cooling rack. Cool completely. Store in airtight
container.                                  *Makes 3 to 3¹/₂ dozen cookies*

**Tip:** You can use your favorite cookie cutter in place of the star cookie
cutter.

*Cinnamon Stars*

# Sweet Walnut Maple Bars

CRUST

    1 package DUNCAN HINES® Moist Deluxe® Classic Yellow
        Cake Mix, divided

  $^1/_3$ cup butter or margarine, melted

   1 egg

TOPPING

  $1^1/_3$ cups MRS. BUTTERWORTH'S® Maple Syrup

   3 eggs

  $^1/_3$ cup firmly packed light brown sugar

  $^1/_2$ teaspoon maple flavoring or vanilla extract

   1 cup chopped walnuts

1. Preheat oven to 350°F. Grease 13×9×2-inch pan.

2. For crust, reserve $^2/_3$ cup cake mix; set aside. Combine remaining cake mix, melted butter and egg in large bowl. Stir until thoroughly blended. (Mixture will be crumbly.) Press into prepared pan. Bake at 350°F for 15 to 20 minutes or until light golden brown.

3. For topping, combine reserved cake mix, maple syrup, eggs, brown sugar and maple flavoring in large bowl. Beat at low speed with electric mixer for 3 minutes. Pour over crust. Sprinkle with walnuts. Bake at 350°F for 30 to 35 minutes or until filling is set. Cool completely. Cut into bars. Store leftover cookie bars in refrigerator. *Makes 24 bars*

*Sweet Walnut Maple Bars*

# Chocolate Almond Biscotti

1 package DUNCAN HINES® Moist Deluxe® Dark Chocolate
   Cake Mix
1 cup all-purpose flour
$^1/_2$ cup butter or margarine, melted
2 eggs
1 teaspoon almond extract
$^1/_2$ cup chopped almonds
   White chocolate, melted (optional)

1. Preheat oven to 350°F. Line 2 baking sheets with parchment paper.

2. Combine cake mix, flour, butter, eggs and almond extract in large bowl. Beat at low speed with electric mixer until well blended; stir in almonds. Divide dough in half. Shape each half into 12×2-inch log; place logs on prepared baking sheets. (Bake logs separately.)

3. Bake at 350°F for 30 to 35 minutes or until toothpick inserted in centers comes out clean. Remove logs from oven; cool on baking sheets 15 minutes. Using serrated knife, cut logs into $^1/_2$-inch slices. Arrange slices on baking sheets. Bake biscotti 10 minutes. Remove to cooling racks; cool completely.

4. Dip one end of each biscotti in melted white chocolate, if desired. Allow white chocolate to set at room temperature before storing biscotti in airtight container.                    *Makes about 2$^1/_2$ dozen cookies*

*Chocolate Almond Biscotti*

# Fudgy Hazelnut Brownies

1 (21-ounce) package DUNCAN HINES® Chewy Fudge
   Brownie Mix
2 eggs
¹/₂ cup vegetable oil
¹/₄ cup water
1 cup chopped toasted hazelnuts
1 cup semisweet chocolate chips
1 cup DUNCAN HINES® Dark Chocolate Frosting
3 squares white chocolate, melted

1. Preheat oven to 350°F. Grease bottom only of 13×9-inch
baking pan.

2. Combine brownie mix, eggs, oil and water in large bowl. Stir with spoon
until well blended, about 50 strokes. Stir in hazelnuts and chocolate chips.
Spread in prepared pan. Bake at 350°F for 25 to 30 minutes or until set.
Cool completely.

3. Heat frosting in microwave oven at HIGH (100% power) for
15 seconds or until thin; stir well. Spread over brownies. Spoon dollops of
white chocolate over chocolate frosting; marble white chocolate through
frosting. Cool completely. Cut into bars.                    *Makes 24 brownies*

*Fudgy Hazelnut Brownies*

# Spicy Oatmeal Raisin Cookies

    1 package DUNCAN HINES® Moist Deluxe® Spice Cake Mix
    4 egg whites
    1 cup uncooked quick-cooking oats (not instant or old-fashioned)
    1/2 cup vegetable oil
    1/2 cup raisins

1. Preheat oven to 350°F. Grease baking sheets.

2. Combine cake mix, egg whites, oats and oil in large mixing bowl. Beat at low speed with electric mixer until blended. Stir in raisins. Drop by rounded teaspoonfuls onto prepared baking sheets.

3. Bake at 350°F for 7 to 9 minutes or until lightly browned. Cool 1 minute on baking sheets. Remove to cooling racks; cool completely.

*Makes about 4 dozen cookies*

# Easy Lemon Cookies

    1 package DUNCAN HINES® Moist Deluxe® Lemon Cake Mix
    2 eggs
    1/2 cup vegetable oil
    1 teaspoon grated lemon peel
    Pecan halves for garnish

1. Preheat oven to 350°F.

2. Combine cake mix, eggs, oil and lemon peel in large bowl. Stir until thoroughly blended. Drop by rounded teaspoonfuls 2 inches apart onto ungreased baking sheets. Press pecan half into center of each cookie.

**3.** Bake at 350°F for 9 to 11 minutes or until edges are light golden brown. Cool 1 minute on baking sheets. Remove to wire racks. Cool completely. Store in airtight container.                   *Makes 4 dozen cookies*

**Tip:** You can substitute whole almonds or walnut halves for the pecan halves.

*Easy Lemon Cookies*

# Double Nut Chocolate Chip Cookies

1 package DUNCAN HINES® Moist Deluxe® Classic Yellow
   Cake Mix
1/2 cup butter or margarine, melted
1 egg
1 cup semisweet chocolate chips
1/2 cup finely chopped pecans
1 cup sliced almonds, divided

1. Preheat oven to 375°F. Grease baking sheets.

2. Combine cake mix, butter and egg in large bowl. Mix at low speed with electric mixer until just blended. Stir in chocolate chips, pecans and 1/4 cup almonds. Shape rounded tablespoonfuls of dough into balls. Place remaining 3/4 cup almonds in shallow bowl. Press tops of cookies into almonds. Place 1 inch apart on prepared baking sheets.

3. Bake at 375°F for 9 to 11 minutes or until lightly browned. Cool 2 minutes on baking sheets. Remove to cooling racks.

*Makes 3 to 3 1/2 dozen cookies*

*Double Nut Chocolate Chip Cookies*

# Coconut Clouds

2²/₃ cups flaked coconut, divided
1 package DUNCAN HINES® Moist Deluxe® Classic Yellow
    Cake Mix
1 egg
¹/₂ cup vegetable oil
¹/₄ cup water
1 teaspoon almond extract

1. Preheat oven to 350°F. Reserve 1¹/₃ cups coconut in medium bowl; set aside.

2. Combine cake mix, egg, oil, water and almond extract in large bowl. Beat at low speed with electric mixer. Stir in remaining 1¹/₃ cups coconut. Drop rounded teaspoonfuls of dough into reserved coconut. Roll to cover lightly. Place balls 2 inches apart on ungreased baking sheet. Repeat with remaining dough. Bake at 350°F for 10 to 12 minutes or until light golden brown. Cool 1 minute on baking sheets. Remove to cooling racks. Cool completely. Store in airtight container.    *Makes 3¹/₂ dozen cookies*

**Cook's Note:** To save time when forming dough into balls, use a 1-inch spring-operated cookie scoop. Spring-operated cookie scoops are available at kitchen specialty shops.

*Coconut Clouds*

# Double Mint Brownies

1 (21-ounce) package DUNCAN HINES® Family-Style Chewy
    Recipe Fudge Brownie Mix

1 egg

⅓ cup water

⅓ cup vegetable oil plus additional for greasing

½ teaspoon peppermint extract

24 chocolate-covered peppermint patties (1½ inches each)

1 cup confectioners' sugar, divided

4 teaspoons milk, divided

    Red food coloring

    Green food coloring

1. Preheat oven to 350°F. Grease bottom only of 13×9×2-inch pan.
Combine brownie mix, egg, water, oil and peppermint extract in large
bowl. Stir with spoon until well blended, about 50 strokes. Spread in
prepared pan. Bake brownies following package directions. Place
peppermint patties on warm brownies. Cool completely.

2. Combine ½ cup confectioners' sugar, 2 teaspoons milk and 1 drop red
food coloring in small bowl. Stir until smooth. Place in small resealable
plastic bag; set aside. Repeat with remaining ½ cup confectioners' sugar,
remaining 2 teaspoons milk and 1 drop green food coloring. Cut pinpoint
hole in bottom corner of each bag. Drizzle pink and green glazes over
brownies as shown. Allow glazes to set before cutting into bars.

*Makes 24 brownies*

**Tip:** To prevent overdone edges and underdone center, wrap foil strips
around outside edges of pan (do not cover bottom or top). Bake as
directed above.

*Double Mint Brownies*

# Orange Pecan Gems

1 package DUNCAN HINES® Moist Deluxe® Orange Supreme
   Cake Mix

1 container (8 ounces) vanilla low fat yogurt

1 egg

2 tablespoons butter or margarine, softened

1 cup finely chopped pecans

1 cup pecan halves

1. Preheat oven to 350°F. Grease baking sheets.

2. Combine cake mix, yogurt, egg, butter and chopped pecans in large
bowl. Beat at low speed with electric mixer until blended. Drop by rounded
teaspoonfuls 2 inches apart onto prepared baking sheets. Press pecan half
onto center of each cookie. Bake at 350°F for 11 to 13 minutes or until
golden brown. Cool 1 minute on baking sheets. Remove to cooling racks.
Cool completely. Store in airtight container.

*Makes 4$^1$/$_2$ to 5 dozen cookies*

# Chocolate Peanut Butter Cookies

1 package DUNCAN HINES® Moist Deluxe® Devil's Food
   Cake Mix

$^3$/$_4$ cup crunchy peanut butter

2 eggs

2 tablespoons milk

1 cup candy-coated peanut butter pieces

1. Preheat oven to 350°F. Grease baking sheets.

2. Combine cake mix, peanut butter, eggs and milk in large mixing bowl. Beat at low speed with electric mixer until blended. Stir in peanut butter pieces.

3. Drop dough by slightly rounded tablespoonfuls onto prepared baking sheets. Bake 7 to 9 minutes or until lightly browned. Cool 2 minutes on baking sheets. Remove to cooling racks.

*Makes about 3¹/₂ dozen cookies*

**Tip:** You can use 1 cup peanut butter chips in place of candy-coated peanut butter pieces.

*Chocolate Peanut Butter Cookies*

# Cakes, Breads & More

Duncan Hines® will help you create
magical cakes and breads. You'll find
recipes for shortcake, upside-down cake,
layer cake and so much more in flavors
from very berry to cool key lime.

# Double Berry Layer Cake

1 package DUNCAN HINES® Moist Deluxe® Strawberry
  Supreme Cake Mix
$^2/_3$ cup strawberry jam, divided
$2^1/_2$ cups fresh blueberries, rinsed, drained and divided
1 container (8 ounces) frozen whipped topping, thawed and
  divided
Fresh strawberry slices for garnish

1. Preheat oven to 350°F. Grease and flour two 9-inch round cake pans.

2. Prepare, bake and cool cake following package directions for basic recipe.

3. Place one cake layer on serving plate. Spread with $^1/_3$ cup strawberry jam. Arrange 1 cup blueberries on jam. Spread half the whipped topping to within $^1/_2$ inch of cake edge. Place second cake layer on top. Repeat with remaining $^1/_3$ cup strawberry jam, 1 cup blueberries and remaining whipped topping. Garnish with strawberry slices and remaining $^1/_2$ cup blueberries. Refrigerate until ready to serve.     *Makes 12 servings*

**Tip:** For best results, cut cake with serrated knife; clean knife after each slice.

# Blueberry Orange Muffins

1 package DUNCAN HINES® Bakery-Style Wild Maine
    Blueberry Muffin Mix
$^{1}/_{2}$ cup orange juice
2 egg whites
1 teaspoon grated orange peel

1. Preheat oven to 400°F. Grease 2$^{1}/_{2}$-inch muffin cups (or use paper liners).

2. Rinse blueberries from Mix with cold water and drain.

3. Empty muffin mix into large bowl. Break up any lumps. Add orange juice, egg whites and orange peel. Stir until moistened, about 50 strokes. Fold blueberries gently into batter.

4. For large muffins, fill cups two-thirds full. Bake at 400°F for 18 to 21 minutes or until toothpick inserted into centers comes out clean. (For medium muffins, fill cups half full. Bake at 400°F for 16 to 19 minutes or until toothpick inserted into centers comes out clean.) Cool in pan 5 to 10 minutes. Carefully loosen muffins from pan. Remove to cooling racks. Serve warm or cool completely.         *Makes 8 large or 12 medium muffins*

**Tip:** Freeze extra grated orange peel for future use.

# Peachy Cinnamon Coffeecake

1 can (8$^{1}/_{4}$ ounces) juice packed sliced yellow cling peaches
1 package DUNCAN HINES® Bakery-Style Cinnamon Swirl
    Muffin Mix
1 egg

**1.** Preheat oven to 400°F. Grease 8-inch square or 9-inch round pan.

**2.** Drain peaches, reserving juice. Add water to reserved juice to equal ¾ cup liquid. Chop peaches.

**3.** Combine muffin mix, egg and ¾ cup peach liquid in medium bowl; fold in peaches. Pour batter into prepared pan. Knead swirl packet 10 seconds before opening. Squeeze contents onto top of batter and swirl with knife. Sprinkle topping over batter. Bake at 400°F for 28 to 33 minutes for 8-inch pan (or 20 to 25 minutes for 9-inch pan) or until golden. Serve warm. *Makes 9 servings*

*Peachy Cinnamon Coffeecake*

# Butter Pecan Banana Cake

CAKE

>  1 package DUNCAN HINES® Moist Deluxe® Butter Recipe
>  Golden Cake Mix
>
>  4 eggs
>
>  1 cup mashed ripe bananas (about 3 medium)
>
>  ³/₄ cup vegetable oil
>
>  ¹/₂ cup granulated sugar
>
>  ¹/₄ cup milk
>
>  1 teaspoon vanilla extract
>
>  1 cup chopped pecans

FROSTING

>  1 cup coarsely chopped pecans
>
>  ¹/₄ cup butter or margarine
>
>  1 container DUNCAN HINES® Vanilla Frosting

1. Preheat oven to 325°F. Grease and flour 10-inch Bundt or tube pan.

2. For cake, combine cake mix, eggs, bananas, oil, sugar, milk and vanilla extract in large mixing bowl. Beat at low speed with electric mixer until moistened. Beat at medium speed for 2 minutes. Stir in 1 cup chopped pecans. Pour into prepared pan. Bake 50 to 60 minutes or until toothpick inserted in center comes out clean. Cool in pan 25 minutes. Invert onto cooling rack. Cool completely.

3. For frosting, place 1 cup coarsely chopped pecans and butter in skillet. Cook on medium heat, stirring until pecans are toasted. Combine nut mixture and frosting in small bowl. Cool until spreading consistency. Frost cake.                    *Makes 12 to 16 servings*

*Butter Pecan Banana Cake*

# Luscious Key Lime Cake

## CAKE

1 package DUNCAN HINES® Moist Deluxe® Lemon Supreme
    Cake Mix

1 package (4-serving size) lemon instant pudding and pie
    filling mix

4 eggs

1 cup vegetable oil

$^3/_4$ cup water

$^1/_4$ cup Key lime juice (see Tip)

## GLAZE

2 cups confectioners' sugar

$^1/_3$ cup Key lime juice

2 tablespoons water

2 tablespoons butter or margarine, melted

Additional confectioners' sugar

Lime slices for garnish

Fresh strawberry slices for garnish (optional)

1. Preheat oven to 350°F. Grease and flour 10-inch Bundt or tube pan.

2. For cake, combine cake mix, pudding mix, eggs, oil, $^3/_4$ cup water and $^1/_4$ cup Key lime juice in large bowl. Beat at low speed with electric mixer until moistened. Beat at medium speed 2 minutes. Pour into pan. Bake at 350°F 50 to 60 minutes or until toothpick inserted in center comes out clean. Cool in pan 25 minutes. Remove cake from pan onto cooling rack. Return cake to pan. Poke holes in top of warm cake with toothpick or long-tined fork.

3. For glaze, combine 2 cups confectioners' sugar, $^1/_3$ cup Key lime juice, 2 tablespoons water and melted butter in medium bowl. Pour slowly over top of warm cake. Cool completely. Invert onto serving plate. Dust with additional confectioners' sugar. Garnish with lime slices and strawberry slices, if desired.  *Makes 12 to 16 servings*

**Tip:** Fresh or bottled lime juice may be substituted for the Key lime juice.

# Cranberry Cobbler

    2 cans (16 ounces each) sliced peaches in light syrup, drained
    1 can (16 ounces) whole berry cranberry sauce
    1 package DUNCAN HINES® Cinnamon Swirl Muffin Mix
$^1/_2$ cup chopped pecans
$^1/_3$ cup butter or margarine, melted
    Whipped topping or ice cream

1. Preheat oven to 350°F.

2. Cut peach slices in half lengthwise. Combine peach slices and cranberry sauce in *ungreased* 9-inch square pan. Knead swirl packet from Mix for 10 seconds. Squeeze contents evenly over fruit.

3. Combine muffin mix, contents of topping packet from Mix and pecans in large bowl. Add melted butter. Stir until thoroughly blended (mixture will be crumbly). Sprinkle crumb mixture over fruit. Bake 40 to 45 minutes or until lightly browned and bubbly. Serve warm with whipped topping.  *Makes 9 servings*

**Tip:** Store leftovers in the refrigerator. Reheat in microwave oven to serve warm.

# Strawberry Shortcake

CAKE

    1 package DUNCAN HINES® Moist Deluxe® French Vanilla
        Cake Mix

    3 eggs

  1 ¼ cups water

    ½ cup butter or margarine, softened

FILLING AND TOPPING

    2 cups whipping cream, chilled

    ⅓ cup sugar

    ½ teaspoon vanilla extract

    1 quart fresh strawberries, rinsed, drained and sliced

    Mint leaves for garnish

1. Preheat oven to 350°F. Grease two 9-inch round cake pans with butter
or margarine. Sprinkle bottom and sides with granulated sugar.

2. For cake, combine cake mix, eggs, water and butter in large bowl. Beat
at low speed with electric mixer until moistened. Beat at medium speed for
2 minutes. Pour into prepared pans. Bake at 350°F for 30 to 35 minutes
or until toothpick inserted in center comes out clean. Cool in pan
10 minutes. Invert onto cooling rack. Cool completely.

**3.** For filling and topping, place whipping cream, sugar and vanilla extract in large bowl. Beat with electric mixer on high speed until stiff peaks form. Reserve $1/3$ cup for garnish. Place one cake layer on serving plate. Spread with half of whipped cream and half of sliced strawberries. Place second layer on top of strawberries. Spread with remaining whipping cream and top with remaining strawberries. Dollop with reserved $1/2$ cup whipped cream and garnish with mint leaves. Refrigerate until ready to serve.                                    *Makes 12 servings*

*Strawberry Shortcake*

# Lemon Bars

1 package DUNCAN HINES® Moist Deluxe® Lemon Supreme
   Cake Mix
3 eggs, divided
$^1/_3$ cup butter-flavor shortening
$^1/_2$ cup granulated sugar
$^1/_4$ cup lemon juice
2 teaspoons grated lemon peel
$^1/_2$ teaspoon baking powder
$^1/_4$ teaspoon salt
   Confectioners' sugar

1. Preheat oven to 350°F.

2. Combine cake mix, 1 egg and shortening in large mixing bowl. Beat at low speed with electric mixer until crumbs form. Reserve 1 cup. Pat remaining mixture lightly into *ungreased* 13×9-inch pan. Bake at 350°F for 15 minutes or until lightly browned.

3. Combine remaining 2 eggs, granulated sugar, lemon juice, lemon peel, baking powder and salt in medium mixing bowl. Beat at medium speed with electric mixer until light and foamy. Pour over hot crust. Sprinkle with reserved crumb mixture.

4. Bake at 350°F for 15 minutes or until lightly browned. Sprinkle with confectioners' sugar. Cool in pan. Cut into bars.     *Makes 30 to 32 bars*

Tip: These bars are also delicious using Duncan Hines® Moist Deluxe® Classic Yellow Cake Mix.

*Lemon Bars*

# Pineapple Upside-Down Cake

TOPPING

  $^{1}/_{2}$ cup butter or margarine

  1 cup firmly packed brown sugar

  1 can (20 ounces) pineapple slices, well drained

    Maraschino cherries, drained and halved

    Walnut halves


CAKE

  1 package DUNCAN HINES® Moist Deluxe® Pineapple Supreme
    Cake Mix

  1 package (4-serving size) vanilla-flavor instant pudding and
    pie filling mix

  4 eggs

  1 cup water

  $^{1}/_{2}$ cup oil

1. Preheat oven to 350°F.

2. For topping, melt butter over low heat in 12-inch cast-iron skillet or skillet with oven-proof handle. Remove from heat. Stir in brown sugar. Spread to cover bottom of skillet. Arrange pineapple slices, maraschino cherries and walnut halves in skillet. Set aside.

**3.** For cake, combine cake mix, pudding mix, eggs, water and oil in large mixing bowl. Beat at medium speed with electric mixer for 2 minutes. Pour batter evenly over fruit in skillet. Bake at 350°F for 1 hour or until toothpick inserted in center comes out clean. Invert onto serving plate.

*Makes 12 to 16 servings*

**Tip:** Cake can be made in a 13×9×2-inch pan. Bake at 350°F for 45 to 55 minutes or until toothpick inserted in center comes out clean. Cake is also delicious using Duncan Hines® Moist Deluxe® Yellow Cake Mix.

*Pineapple Upside Down Cake*

# Orange Cinnamon Swirl Bread

BREAD

   1 package DUNCAN HINES® Bakery-Style Cinnamon Swirl
      Muffin Mix

   1 egg

   $^2/_3$ cup orange juice

   1 tablespoon grated orange peel


ORANGE GLAZE

   $^1/_2$ cup confectioners' sugar

   2 to 3 teaspoons orange juice

   1 teaspoon grated orange peel

      Quartered orange slices for garnish (optional)

1. Preheat oven to 350°F. Grease and flour $8^1/_2 \times 4^1/_2 \times 2^1/_2$-inch
loaf pan.

2. For bread, combine muffin mix and contents of topping packet from
mix in large bowl. Break up any lumps. Add egg, $^2/_3$ cup orange juice and
1 tablespoon orange peel. Stir until moistened, about 50 strokes. Knead
swirl packet from mix for 10 seconds before opening. Squeeze contents on
top of batter. Swirl into batter with knife or spatula, folding from bottom
of bowl to get an even swirl. *Do not completely mix in.* Pour into prepared
pan. Bake at 350°F for 55 to 60 minutes or until toothpick inserted in
center comes out clean. Cool in pan 10 minutes. Loosen loaf from pan.
Invert onto cooling rack. Turn right side up. Cool completely.

3. For orange glaze, place confectioners' sugar in small bowl. Add orange
juice, 1 teaspoon at a time, stirring until smooth and of desired
consistency. Stir in 1 teaspoon orange peel. Drizzle over loaf. Garnish
with orange slices, if desired.                    *Makes 1 loaf (12 slices)*

*Orange Cinnamon Swirl Bread*

# Blueberry Cheesecake Bars

1 package DUNCAN HINES® Bakery-Style Blueberry Streusel
    Muffin Mix

$^{1}/_{4}$ cup cold butter or margarine

$^{1}/_{3}$ cup finely chopped pecans

1 package (8 ounces) cream cheese, softened

$^{1}/_{2}$ cup sugar

1 egg

3 tablespoons lemon juice

1 teaspoon grated lemon peel

1. Preheat oven to 350°F. Grease 9-inch square baking pan.

2. Rinse blueberries from Mix with cold water and drain; set aside.

3. Place muffin mix in medium bowl; cut in butter with pastry blender or two knives. Stir in pecans. Press into bottom of prepared pan. Bake at 350°F for 15 minutes or until set.

4. Combine cream cheese and sugar in medium bowl. Beat until smooth. Add egg, lemon juice and lemon peel. Beat well. Spread over baked crust. Sprinkle with blueberries. Sprinkle topping packet from Mix over blueberries. Return to oven. Bake at 350°F for 35 to 40 minutes or until filling is set. Cool completely. Refrigerate until ready to serve. Cut into bars.

*Makes about 16 bars*

# Strawberry Stripe Refrigerator Cake

CAKE

> 1 package DUNCAN HINES® Moist Deluxe® Classic White
>   Cake Mix
> 2 packages (10 ounces) frozen sweetened strawberry slices, thawed

TOPPING

> 1 package (4-serving size) vanilla-flavor instant pudding and pie
>   filling mix
> 1 cup milk
> 1 cup whipping cream, whipped
>   Fresh strawberries for garnish (optional)

1. Preheat oven to 350°F. Grease and flour 13×9×2-inch pan.

2. For cake, prepare, bake and cool following package directions. Poke holes 1 inch apart in top of cake using handle of wooden spoon. Purée thawed strawberries with juice in blender or food processor. Spoon evenly over top of cake, allowing mixture to soak into holes.

3. For topping, combine pudding mix and milk in large bowl. Stir until smooth. Fold in whipped cream. Spread over cake. Decorate with fresh strawberries, if desired. Refrigerate at least 4 hours.

*Makes 12 to 16 servings*

**Tip:** For a Neapolitan Refrigerator Cake, replace the White Cake Mix with Duncan Hines® Moist Deluxe® Devil's Food Cake Mix and follow directions listed above.

# Chocolate Banana Cake

CAKE

> 1 package DUNCAN HINES® Moist Deluxe® Devil's Food
> Cake Mix
>
> 3 eggs
>
> 1 1/3 cups milk
>
> 1/2 cup vegetable oil

TOPPING

> 1 package (4-serving size) banana cream instant pudding and
> pie filling mix
>
> 1 cup milk
>
> 1 cup whipping cream, whipped
>
> 1 medium banana
>
> Lemon juice
>
> Chocolate sprinkles for garnish

1. Preheat oven to 350°F. Grease and flour 13×9×2-inch pan.

2. For cake, combine cake mix, eggs, milk and oil in large bowl. Beat at low speed with electric mixer until moistened. Beat at medium speed 2 minutes. Pour into pan. Bake at 350°F 35 to 38 minutes or until toothpick inserted in center comes out clean. Cool completely.

3. For topping, combine pudding mix and milk in large bowl. Stir until smooth. Fold in whipped cream. Spread on top of cooled cake. Slice banana; dip in lemon juice, arrange on top. Garnish with chocolate sprinkles. Refrigerate until ready to serve.      *Makes 12 to 16 servings*

**Tip:** A wire whisk is a great utensil to use when making instant pudding. It quickly eliminates all lumps.

*Chocolate Banana Cake*

# Berry Filled Muffins

    1 package DUNCAN HINES® Bakery-Style Wild Maine
        Blueberry Muffin Mix
    1 egg
    $^1/_2$ cup water
    $^1/_4$ cup strawberry jam
    2 tablespoons sliced natural almonds

1. Preheat oven to 400°F. Place 8 (2$^1/_2$-inch) paper or foil liners in muffin cups; set aside.

2. Rinse blueberries from Mix with cold water and drain.

3. Empty muffin mix into bowl. Break up any lumps. Add egg and water. Stir until moistened, about 50 strokes. Fill cups half full with batter.

4. Fold blueberries into jam. Spoon on top of batter in each cup. Spread gently. Cover with remaining batter. Sprinkle with almonds. Bake at 400°F for 17 to 20 minutes or until set and golden brown. Cool in pan 5 to 10 minutes. Loosen carefully before removing from pan.

*Makes 8 muffins*

# Refreshing Lemon Cake

    1 package DUNCAN HINES® Moist Deluxe® Butter Recipe
        Golden Cake Mix
    1 container DUNCAN HINES® Creamy Home-Style Cream
        Cheese Frosting
    $^3/_4$ cup purchased lemon curd
    Lemon drop candies, crushed for garnish (optional)

1. Preheat oven to 375°F. Grease and flour two 8- or 9-inch round cake pans.

2. Prepare, bake and cool cake following package directions for basic recipe.

3. To assemble, place one cake layer on serving plate. Place ¼ cup Cream Cheese frosting in small resealable plastic bag. Snip off one corner. Pipe a bead of frosting on top of layer around outer edge. Fill remaining area with lemon curd. Top with second cake layer. Spread remaining frosting on sides and top of cake. Garnish top of cake with crushed lemon candies, if desired.                    *Makes 12 to 16 servings*

**Tip:** You can substitute Duncan Hines® Vanilla or Vanilla Buttercream frosting for the Cream Cheese frosting, if desired.

*Refreshing Lemon Cake*

# Carrot Layer Cake

CAKE

>       1 package DUNCAN HINES® Moist Deluxe® Classic Yellow
>          Cake Mix
>       4 eggs
>     1/2 cup vegetable oil
>       3 cups grated carrots
>       1 cup finely chopped nuts
>       2 teaspoons ground cinnamon

CREAM CHEESE FROSTING

>       1 package (8 ounces) cream cheese, softened
>     1/4 cup butter or margarine, softened
>       2 teaspoons vanilla extract
>       4 cups confectioners' sugar

1. Preheat oven to 350°F. Grease and flour two 8- or 9-inch round baking pans.

2. For cake, combine cake mix, eggs, oil, carrots, nuts and cinnamon in large bowl. Beat at low speed with electric mixer until moistened. Beat at medium speed for 2 minutes. Pour into prepared pans. Bake at 350°F for 35 to 40 minutes or until toothpick inserted in centers comes out clean. Cool.

3. For cream cheese frosting, place cream cheese, butter and vanilla extract in large bowl. Beat at low speed until smooth and creamy. Add confectioners' sugar gradually, beating until smooth. Add more sugar to thicken, or milk or water to thin frosting, as needed. Fill and frost cooled cake. Garnish with whole pecans. *Makes 12 to 16 servings*

*Carrot Layer Cake*

# INDEX

**Almond**
Chocolate Almond Biscotti, 38
Chocolate Almond Confection Cake, 16
Double Nut Chocolate Chip Cookies, 44

**Banana**
Banana Fudge Layer Cake, 14
Banana Split Cake, 104
Butter Pecan Banana Cake, 56
Chocolate Banana Cake, 70
Berry Filled Muffins, 72
**Biscotti:** Chocolate Almond Biscotti, 38
**Blueberry**
Berry Filled Muffins, 72
Blueberry Cheesecake Bars, 68
Blueberry Orange Muffins, 54
Double Berry Layer Cake, 53
**Breads**
Coconut Chocolate Chip Loaf, 22
Orange Cinnamon Swirl Bread, 66
**Brownies & Bar Cookies**
Blueberry Cheesecake Bars, 68
Cindy's Fudgy Brownies, 25
Double Chocolate Chewies, 18
Double Mint Brownies, 48
Fudgy Hazelnut Brownies, 40
Lemon Bars, 62
Sweet Walnut Maple Bars, 36
**Bundt & Tube Cakes**
Butter Pecan Banana Cake, 56
Chocolate Almond Confection Cake, 16
Chocolate Streusel Cake, 12

**Bundt & Tube Cakes**
(continued)
Luscious Key Lime Cake, 58
Triple Chocolate Fantasy, 24
Butter Pecan Banana Cake, 56

**Cakes**
Carrot Layer Cake, 74
Chocolate Banana Cake, 70
Pineapple Upside-Down Cake, 64
Strawberry Stripe Refrigerator Cake, 69
**Candy**
Chocolate Oat Chewies, 31
Chocolate Peanut Butter Cookies, 50
Double Mint Brownies, 48
Truffles, 17
Carrot Layer Cake, 74
**Cheesecakes**
Blueberry Cheesecake Bars, 68
Chocolate Chip Cheesecake, 20
**Cherry**
Chocolate Cherry Torte, 10
Chocolate Almond Biscotti, 38
Chocolate Almond Confection Cake, 16
Chocolate Banana Cake, 70
Chocolate Cherry Torte, 10
**Chocolate Chips**
Chocolate Chip Cheesecake, 20
Cindy's Fudgy Brownies, 25
Coconut Chocolate Chip Loaf, 22
Double Chocolate Chewies, 18
Double Nut Chocolate Chip Cookies, 44
Fudgy Hazelnut Brownies, 40
Triple Chocolate Fantasy, 24
Truffles, 17
Chocolate Cream Torte, 28

Chocolate Oat Chewies, 31
Chocolate Peanut Butter Cookies, 50
Chocolate Peanut Butter Cups, 7
Chocolate Streusel Cake, 12
Chocolate Toffee Cream Cake, 90
Chocolate Toffee Crunch Fantasy, 26
Cindy's Fudgy Brownies, 25
Cinnamon Stars, 34
**Cobblers & Shortcakes**
Cranberry Cobbler, 59
Strawberry Shortcake, 60
**Coconut**
Chocolate Oat Chewies, 31
Coconut Chocolate Chip Loaf, 22
Coconut Clouds, 46
Upside-Down German Chocolate Cake, 8
**Coffeecakes:** Peachy Cinnamon Coffeecake, 54
**Cranberry:** Cranberry Cobbler, 59
**Cream Cheese**
Blueberry Cheesecake Bars, 68
Carrot Layer Cake, 74
Chocolate Chip Cheesecake, 20
Chocolate Cream Torte, 28
Upside-Down German Chocolate Cake, 8
**Cupcakes"** Chocolate Peanut Butter Cups, 7

Double Berry Layer Cake, 53
Double Chocolate Chewies, 18
Double Mint Brownies, 48
Double Nut Chocolate Chip Cookies, 44

Easy Lemon Cookies, 42

Fudgy Hazelnut Brownies, 40

**Hazelnuts:** Fudgy Hazelnut Brownies, 40
**Key Lime:** Luscious Key Lime Cake, 58
**Layer Cakes**
Banana Fudge Layer Cake, 14
Carrot Layer Cake, 74
Chocolate Toffee Crunch Fantasy, 26
Double Berry Layer Cake, 53
Refreshing Lemon Cake, 72
**Lemon**
Easy Lemon Cookies, 42
Lemon Bars, 62
Refreshing Lemon Cake, 72
Luscious Key Lime Cake, 58

**Maple:** Sweet Walnut Maple Bars, 36
**Mint:** Double Mint Brownies, 48
**Muffins**
Berry Filled Muffins, 72
Blueberry Orange Muffins, 54

**Nuts** (see also individual listings)
Carrot Layer Cake, 74
Double Chocolate Chewies, 18

**Oats**
Chocolate Oat Chewies, 31
Spicy Oatmeal Raisin Cookies, 42
**Orange**
Blueberry Orange Muffins, 54
Orange Cinnamon Swirl Bread, 66
Orange Pecan Gems, 50

**Peaches**
Cranberry Cobbler, 59
Peachy Cinnamon Coffeecake, 54
Peachy Cinnamon Coffeecake, 54

**Peanut Butter**
Chocolate Peanut Butter Cookies, 50
Chocolate Peanut Butter Cups, 7
**Pecans**
Butter Pecan Banana Cake, 56
Chocolate Cream Torte, 28
Chocolate Streusel Cake, 12
Cindy's Fudgy Brownies, 25
Cranberry Cobbler, 59
Double Nut Chocolate Chip Cookies, 44
Orange Pecan Gems, 50
Truffles, 17
Upside-Down German Chocolate Cake, 8
**Pineapple:** Pineapple Upside-Down Cake, 64
Pinwheel Cookies, 32

Quick Rocky Road Cake, 120

**Raisins:** Spicy Oatmeal Raisin Cookies, 42
Refreshing Lemon Cake, 72

Spicy Oatmeal Raisin Cookies, 42
**Strawberry**
Double Berry Layer Cake, 53
Strawberry Shortcake, 60
Strawberry Stripe Refrigerator Cake, 69
**Streusel:** Chocolate Streusel Cake, 12
Sweet Walnut Maple Bars, 36

**Toffee:** Chocolate Toffee Crunch Fantasy, 26
**Tortes**
Chocolate Cherry Torte, 10
Chocolate Cream Torte, 28
Triple Chocolate Fantasy, 24
Truffles, 17

Upside-Down German Chocolate Cake, 8

**Walnuts**
Sweet Walnut Maple Bars, 36
Triple Chocolate Fantasy, 24
**Whipped Topping**
Chocolate Cherry Torte, 10
Chocolate Streusel Cake, 12
Double Berry Layer Cake, 53
**Whipping Cream**
Chocolate Banana Cake, 70
Chocolate Cream Torte, 28
Chocolate Toffee Crunch Fantasy, 26
Strawberry Shortcake, 60
Strawberry Stripe Refrigerator Cake, 69
**White Chocolate**
Fudgy Hazelnut Brownies, 40
Triple Chocolate Fantasy, 24

**Yogurt:** Orange Pecan Gems, 50

## VOLUME MEASUREMENTS (dry)

$^1/_8$ teaspoon = 0.5 mL
$^1/_4$ teaspoon = 1 mL
$^1/_2$ teaspoon = 2 mL
$^3/_4$ teaspoon = 4 mL
1 teaspoon = 5 mL
1 tablespoon = 15 mL
2 tablespoons = 30 mL
$^1/_4$ cup = 60 mL
$^1/_3$ cup = 75 mL
$^1/_2$ cup = 125 mL
$^2/_3$ cup = 150 mL
$^3/_4$ cup = 175 mL
1 cup = 250 mL
2 cups = 1 pint = 500 mL
3 cups = 750 mL
4 cups = 1 quart = 1 L

## VOLUME MEASUREMENTS (fluid)

1 fluid ounce (2 tablespoons) = 30 mL
4 fluid ounces ($^1/_2$ cup) = 125 mL
8 fluid ounces (1 cup) = 250 mL
12 fluid ounces (1$^1/_2$ cups) = 375 mL
16 fluid ounces (2 cups) = 500 mL

## WEIGHTS (mass)

$^1/_2$ ounce = 15 g
1 ounce = 30 g
3 ounces = 90 g
4 ounces = 120 g
8 ounces = 225 g
10 ounces = 285 g
12 ounces = 360 g
16 ounces = 1 pound = 450 g

## DIMENSIONS

$^1/_{16}$ inch = 2 mm
$^1/_8$ inch = 3 mm
$^1/_4$ inch = 6 mm
$^1/_2$ inch = 1.5 cm
$^3/_4$ inch = 2 cm
1 inch = 2.5 cm

## OVEN TEMPERATURES

250°F = 120°C
275°F = 140°C
300°F = 150°C
325°F = 160°C
350°F = 180°C
375°F = 190°C
400°F = 200°C
425°F = 220°C
450°F = 230°C

## BAKING PAN SIZES

| Utensil | Size in Inches/Quarts | Metric Volume | Size in Centimeters |
|---|---|---|---|
| Baking or | 8×8×2 | 2 L | 20×20×5 |
| Cake Pan | 9×9×2 | 2.5 L | 23×23×5 |
| (square or | 12×8×2 | 3 L | 30×20×5 |
| rectangular) | 13×9×2 | 3.5 L | 33×23×5 |
| Loaf Pan | 8×4×3 | 1.5 L | 20×10×7 |
| | 9×5×3 | 2 L | 23×13×7 |
| Round Layer | 8×1½ | 1.2 L | 20×4 |
| Cake Pan | 9×1½ | 1.5 L | 23×4 |
| Pie Plate | 8×1¼ | 750 mL | 20×3 |
| | 9×1¼ | 1 L | 23×3 |
| Baking Dish | 1 quart | 1 L | — |
| or Casserole | 1½ quart | 1.5 L | — |
| | 2 quart | 2 L | — |